RAVAGE ME

How to Indulge in Your Desires and Avoid the Lunacies of Love, Sex, and Relationships

Mikael Winters & Cheyenne Morgan

Ravage Me

ISBN 978-0-9961444-0-7

Introduction

Living under the guise of a seemingly novice pupil in the adventures of love, sex, and relationships has been no small feat. This coming from a young woman incessantly teased for having a "big nose" (I'm Jewish and African American), being a "nerd," "lame," "unpopular," "not pretty as your little sister," etc. I was not embraced by my peers nor was I regarded by pre-pubescent boys as lust worthy. It was a crappy adolescence existence...until I grew breasts! Then, all of a sudden, I'm being ogled, fondled, and bombarded with a plethora of requests for dates amongst drunken proposals—all from my late teens to my early twenties. Anything after that could be simply characterized as a blur of run-ins with stalkers, romps with mismatched love interests, and *aha* sexual discoveries!

This was my world: the woman with no influence, barely possessing a minced-up ounce of confidence—to speak my peace period! That *was* me. Have you ever struggled with finding the words to convey what you *want* and *don't want*—especially, in the affairs of love? Sex? Relationships? Do you find it difficult to *boldly* ask your significant other to touch your erogenous zones without feeling embarrassed? Ridiculous? Rejected? Are you a codependent magnet and hung over on love addictions? Are you aware of the difference between *acquired* taste and desire?

Upon reading *Ravage Me*, you will identify ways of painting an illustrious canvas with your mouth and how to safeguard the invaluable contents of your heart.

That's why I wrote the book. It originated out of conversations with friends, delved into my past, dabbled into some science, and eventually smacked me on my ass! Then stirred my interest as to why I had to write this—this was me. I became so irritated with popular culture's crude pokes at men and women alike, e.g., "side-piece," "jump-off," etc., all the while people are happily bragging on social media about messy, messy love triangles, yet are *still* unfulfilled in the interpersonal relationship dynamic. I call these people "the coonery brigade." Yes, you can post comments all day about how you laid it down last night and gave head like a champ, but are you truly happy? The shit is ridiculous! Insert my opinion on tastes versus desire, when some people *actually* think they mean the same thing—they don't … well, not in relationships! I'm sooooo biased. Yes, I am as to the way I feel. I'm not a connoisseur, and this book is for those that want "real talk" about the interpersonal relationship dynamic without the flowery imagery or medical-oriented feel. I'm not on that. Whether you're love starved, the significant other of a sexually repressed man or woman, fixated on Hollywood imagery, frozen in bizarre obsessions, or not enjoying the full benefits of the undefiled marriage bed, this book is for you, the one that needs ravaging.

This book is not about how to fix your relationship in thirty days or less or how to heal from past hurts and wounds, although you may find recovery in your journey as you piece together information through your reading. There are thousands of wonderful books in the marketplace about love, sex, and relationships. This book is about one of our most important, yet neglected, human needs: desire. It's about knowing *how* and *when* to speak up—finding your voice.

There's no roundtable of expert opinions, nor are there a bunch of eloquent quotes or case studies from authors on the subject matter. It doesn't bother me when people question my perspective or ideology of interpersonal relationships, being that I'm not even forty years of age. I adhere to the fact that I don't have the relationship-answer mojo! But what I do have are plenty of friends, family, and snarky, fellow church- goers who can help fill in the blanks about inter-personal relationships. These include a close family member, my co-author, Mikael Winters, an author and Atlanta-based playwright. His great wisdom, gained through personal experience, research, and prolific insight in dealing with people, solidifies the core of the interpersonal-relationship content in this book. Mikael Winters makes sure that it's both witty and relevant! I know that this book may be controversial to some audiences. It challenges the status quo about sex, love, and relationships ... and forces you to bite down on your tongue! To step away from rehearsed rules and into wanton abandon. There's nothing complicated about the content—no tests, evaluations, harsh assessments, etc., just an about-face at your life. When you finish reading this book, my hope is that you've grabbed a few tips to get you on a healthy track of indulgence and desire.

Who Is Mikael Winters and Why Did He Decide to Write This Book?

After forty-three years of observation and counseling thousands of couples in relationships—non-married/married-alike—I have witnessed nearly every entrapment known to man, from emotional manipulation to ludicrous love triangles. It was quite disheartening having to witness people destroy decent relationships (well, all weren't decent) over foolishness. Being privy to some of the most sensitive and sometimes dark information shared with me over the years, I preserved it—not to expose people and their pain, but to capture the essence of the relationship dynamic ... to help someone in the future. I myself can attest to the lunacies of interpersonal relationships and later in life learning about giving in to desire. From having been the victim of sexual harassment as a male in my twelve-year tenure as a white-collar worker in corporate America to my personal experience as a youngster at the age of fourteen, being used sexually by older women, my life story intertwines with the ten chapters of this book … *my* secrets of course.

Contents

Fantasy, Hollywood, Mirages

Damn! Look at that chocolate (or vanilla) brotha, abs all greased up, as he's kissing a female starlet ... slowly moving down to the small of her back. Peep the busty brunette: toned body, in a blue bikini and black stilettos, on a white carpet, giving head to an equally attractive man. Getting you hot? Bothered? Isn't Hollywood clever? It's all in the marketing . . . the glitz and the glamour. They could take a high school nerd—be it male or female—and make them look very, *very* appealing! That's not everyday reality.

That's Hollywood. A fantasy ... a mirage.

Growing up, the first image a man has of a woman is his mom. Mom sets the stage for the type of woman her son will come to love or hate. Although Mom walks around with her gravy-stained robe, hair rollers, and rundown slippers, she gets a "pass." Surely, the woman he marries gotta be *"Hollywood Glamour,"* all day every day! Men that have sisters are more understanding of a woman's imperfection; they've seen them without makeup, hair wild, clothes unkempt, etc. On the flip side, men that do *not* have sisters can only see a woman at her best and have an unrealistic expectation that a woman must be perfect at all times!

Fast forward twenty-five to thirty years later, and that young man gets married. He marries a beautiful woman who keeps her hair, nails, body, clothes—all that—on point! The sex is wild and adventurous; she gives it to him *how* he wants and keeps him begging for more. They go out *all* the time. She's *his* show-piece, *his* visually appealing arm candy! He delights in her and she in him. After about— umm—three to four years, (in her mind) she's like: "Shit, I've got this man; fuck all this upkeep!" The decline in her appearance shows up:

- At work
- In public
- At home

This visual alteration is devastating to him! He won't make a big deal about how she looks at work, unless they work in the same office. Being in public with his woman was his favorite pastime! They would go dancing, jog around the block, and eat at eclectic restaurants. He becomes embarrassed by how his woman looks in public and no longer wants to be seen with her. At home, the two kids dominate the arena and his woman's time. When he looks at her, he doesn't feel lustful as he did before. The sexual attraction is gone!

At night time, she dons a purple satin bonnet and some worn-out, two-piece polyester pajamas, trying to cuddle up to him for some nookie. He's repulsed! To attempt to get in the mood, he fantasizes about her former fine ass! She used to be 130 lbs. with a flat stomach, large, supple breasts (a mouthful, he says), and shoulder-length brown hair. But, after she had two kids, her weight jumped from 130 lbs. to 220 lbs.—and that's post-pregnancy from BOTH babies! Damn! What to do here?

Here's a quick fact for the fellas and the ladies: There is an understudy, and he or she is *ready* and *willing* to step in to *your* role and hold down that Hollywood image. Don't think that you're irreplaceable! Every man has a dick, as every woman has a pussy, but neither is created equal. It's not called that good-good for nothing!

The first man that a woman sees is Daddy. He can be skinny, fat, or talk with a lisp—there are *no* flaws in Daddy. She sees him come home from work, spend special Daddy-daughter time with her, and treat her like a princess. He may come home with his clothes smelling of sweat, fingernails dirty, etc., but if he ever had a gift for her, his daughter looked past all that and was all smiles. Thus, Daddy gets a "pass," too! It's "Daddy, Daddy, Daddy!" Women have a tendency to wear that name out!

A good mom teaches her daughter that Daddy works to provide for the family, and that one day, she would have the same in a husband. So that good mom, in turn, also taught the daughter how to maintain her home and how to treat her man. When this woman eventually gets married, the man she meets falls into a side-by-side comparison with Daddy. It's not completely intentional, but if Daddy lavishes her with affection, attention, and gifts, the daughter *is* going to want the same out of a man.

On the contrary, if Daddy was abusive, mean-spirited, or absent, she could possibly attract or repel this type of man. Either way, and at long last, this glorious day has come: She's a *married* woman now! That man is fine! Every chance she gets she's showing him off, too: high school reunions, church, date night. She is gonna do *whatever* it takes to keep his eyes from wandering! Armed with an arsenal of teddies, garter belts, risqué sex toys, and, of course, food and a clean home, she's got this! He's been doing his part, too! Working out at the gym, surprising her with gifts, and taking her on impromptu vacations. As the years go by, he stops exercising, develops type II diabetes, and his six pack turns into a beer belly. He used to get manicures and pedicures with his woman. Don't get it twisted! Men should get pampered, too! It won't take away from a man's masculinity.

Now, when he comes home from work, his clothes reek of gasoline, underneath his nails look like he's been planting crops all day, and … he wants a hug and kiss? What happened to that fine man who had it all together? She begins to fantasize about how she used to nuzzle into the nook of his neck, enjoying the scent of his cologne. As she snaps back into reality, she's truly sad that he has a life-altering disease, but does he have to look the part? What happened? I mean, he had a *way* ... he knew *how* to touch her, but using ragged fingernails while trying to finger her—ouch! Turnoff!

She tries to remain faithful but can't stand bruh at home *not* handling his business. All the while, someone else has caught her eye and is baiting her with attention and affection. This is a "clean-up" man. He does not care that she is married, nor does he care that she has children. He thinks that it's just sex ... *no strings*. He pursues her relentlessly and won't take no for an answer. Eventually, she gives in to her desires. Then, after the fire dies down from that "romance," she returns home, distraught and broken. Who's there to pick up the pieces?

> WARNING: I don't care how bright Hollywood's star is, don't let it outshine *you*! Theirs is a mirage; yours is *real*!

So this is love? "No more condoms!" "I can't wait to get back to the hotel." "How about a threesome?" "Are you into anal?" Damn! This is for the singles, albeit newly monogamous couples. You've barely made it one mile from the concert hall and your new boyfriend is bombarding you with what he wants in the bedroom … not the idyllic utopia you'd hoped for. You're praying this is Mr. Right, so you can stop giving up pussy on the daily. I mean, it is normal for a female to like sex as much as a guy! This chick will probably be scared shitless and leave this guy's sorry ass! What a waste of good lovin'. Just when you get used to someone, they go and fuck up everything! Before you know it, you're back on the "singles strip," trying to find that non-existent mirage of a human being.

Don't get stuck into a vicious cycle of trying to find an "ideal" image; pray that the person has mental stability above anything else. Um, all them other kinks, i.e. finances, attractiveness, sex, etc., can be worked out. You might be sitting at the table across from gap-toothed Tyler, dreading having to kiss him goodnight one day. But, several months later, after the lights go out, you're getting laid, so who gives a fuck?!

Love Starved

She's in a chat room, sharing a picture of her pierced nipples to some random stranger. He just posted a "casual encounters" ad on a social media website. She's recently joined a swingers club *exclusively* for married couples. He's jacking off to the voice of a phone sex operator. What the hell is goin' on here? These are people that are searching for something that is non-existent. The search goes on ... and leads to riskier sexual antics. For example, engaging in sexual orgies with multiple men and women, using asphyxiation, cutting, and vampirism—all to achieve climax. All of these are examples a love-starved individual may use to escape the emotional pain they are experiencing. Then drugs come into play, such as mixing ecstasy and Viagra to achieve what some call a potent sexual high.

If you've ever been in a love-starved situation, you're easy prey for anyone to manipulate and discard like flavorless gum. Really, you say? Yep! The kick-me sign is already on your back. You're a marked target. What usually happens is that a love-starved individual is either in a crappy-ass relationship or reeling from the loss of the supposed "love of their life." However, the love-starved individual that's in a crappy-ass relationship is the most vulnerable; they should be gettin' lovin' elsewhere.

He could be a powerful CEO of a major fortune 500 company yet has a sexually repressed wife. He begins to visit the local library daily, dressed in jeans, a t-shirt, and a baseball cap—totally unrecognizable should any colleagues or business associates see him. Chatting with a female college student who frequents there becomes the daily norm. She's not all that attractive to mainstream society's standards. In fact, she looks more like a wallflower: no makeup, glasses, wears long dresses with a cardigan, and steel-toe boots. The conversation they share about a famous local painter engages them both. One day, she suggests that he briefly stop by her off-campus apartment, as she has some of this artist's work displayed on the wall. Peering around her cramped, yet quaint, living space reminds him of when he was in college as well. Twenty years his senior, this female college student doesn't feel this guy could be her dad—she's just enjoying conversation, a common interest.

Upon leaving, they briefly embrace … and share the joy they had meeting at the library. But this time something is different. The female college student grazes the male CEO's chin with her thumb and forefinger, giving him a soft peck on the lips. Thinking that he would reject her, she mumbles an apology. But, before she can get "sorry" out her mouth, the CEO kisses her back—this time more passionately. She pushes some clothes off the couch, onto the floor, and strips him naked, delighting him with scandalous acts of pleasure!

Sadly, this is the first time in his fifty-one years he's felt this way—fulfilled—both sexually and emotionally with *any* woman, namely his wife. Neither intended for an affair to develop; his tank was empty, and she was all too eager to fill it. In actuality, this act is now the coup de grâce of his marriage—it's over! Not to say the CEO won't leave his wife because he found good lovin', but he'll definitely make it back to her pad for some refills!

In the case of the newly separated female who lost the "love of her life," she's a little more desperate than she is vulnerable. Meet the forty-five-year-old blogger. She ends an eight-year on-again, off-again relationship with her programmer boyfriend who just took a job offer in Oslo, Norway. The breakup shatters her, because this guy was her first *everything*: fuck, long-term relationship, etc. She believed that one day he would marry her, and under the premise of a pending marriage proposal, she gave up her prized virginity to him. Desperate to keep him, she let him use her at a whim for all his sexual fantasies. When the relationship ends, she struggles with depression for six months, until a fellow blogger tells her about a social media site where he hooked up with his new girl.

NOTE: The best way to get over someone is to get *under* someone new!

She isn't used to being alone, so this is her next best thing. A few days after creating a profile, she starts chatting with a guy who happens to live ten miles away from her. Their online chats are tantalizing and hot. Soon, he's asking her to position a webcam so he can watch her finger herself. She is delighted to oblige, as she is *lonely.* He states that his webcam is set, but he's shy about showing his dick on camera. He continues to blow her off with more ridiculous excuses as to why he can't expose himself on camera.

She continues to grant his every request… glad that there is applause at the end. One month later, he states he wants to meet her in person and insists on her being blindfolded. Ignorantly, she goes to an undisclosed location. Once she arrives, she knocks on a door, it opens, and she's unable to see who is on the other side. A voice asks her to turn around—he wants to play "the blindfold game." She agrees, thinking that the blindfold will be removed once she's inside. He immediately guides her to a chair. Once she is sat down, the blindfold is *never removed.* The voice states, "You can never see my face." She is frozen in horror. For several hours, she is raped and eventually released the following day. Embarrassed by her own stupidity, she tells no one. She vows never to search for love online again.

Being love starved is akin to not eating enough; eventually, hunger takes over, and you have to give in. You'll eat just about anything when you're starving! When you're with someone, yet feel starved of their affection, you should let them know—immediately! It makes no sense falling into a depression or some hyper-sensitive mode when you have the opportunity to speak your peace. If the person you're with is unwilling to fulfill your needs or even seek counseling, then it's time to can that relationship! One thing about life and love is true: If you don't love the one you're with, you *will* love the one you're *not* with.

Want You, Think I Need You?

I need you!

If you give me this, we can negotiate . . .

I can do this my damn self!

Dependency, codependency, and interdependency—all building blocks of each other; all taught at an early age. Interspersed in a love relationship, it can be a treacherous thing... especially when all of the players aren't truly vested.

Children are trained at an early age to be dependent on who is caring for them, whether it be a parent, an extended relative, or close family friend. When a baby cries for its mother because he or she is hungry, has a wet diaper, or wants attention, the child is cognizant of the fact that someone is going to attend to his/her need(s). In the next phase, the child is taught independent skills: how to eat with a fork, using the bathroom, tying shoes, etc.

Finally, a child is taught interdependency. If the child has siblings at home, this skill is developed first with learning how to share toys and living space, or cleaning up spills. When the child enters school, the interdependency skill reaches a plateau with the heavy interaction of students, teachers, and other staff. For example: sports, school choirs, plays, debates, band, etc. What is happening is that the child's character is being developed.

Young ladies are trained how to be independent at an early age by their parents. They are trained that they don't *need* a man to complete them. So a smart father would take his daughter out for dinner, buy her flowers, tell her how pretty she is. This allows a daughter to know she doesn't need a man to validate her. If this is not embedded in her mind at an early age, a woman will fall *hard* for the first man that tells her she's "pretty." Now, the hook is in. She'll believe *every* word, longing to be in his presence twenty-four hours a day, seven days a week. If the relationship sours and is not meeting her immediate needs, she falters and now feels betrayed. In a minute, she'll be a stalker, showing up unannounced at his job, at his home, or the places he frequents. She lacks the ability to stop attaching herself to anyone that shows her affection and attention. Her self-esteem is non-existent.

If she's an interdependent woman, then she's loves to barter, trading her body for whatever she deems a valuable exchange from a man (or woman). She doesn't deem herself a prostitute; she scoffs at the thought. She's in *full* control of her mind and body—it's not love she's after. At the end of the day, she only *wants* what *she* wants . . . and is gonna find a way to get it!

Most men are not trained to be sensitive to a woman's needs, nor have they seen an example of a *real* man. If they do not receive this training, more than likely they become desensitized to the needs of others and become selfish and self-centered jackasses. Eventually, most men that are desensitized to the needs of others become physically aggressive and/or verbally abusive.

This behavior is characteristic of both the independent, "I don't give a shit" male and female. Sexually, the man and woman will act out this aggression in the bedroom. The desensitized man doesn't care about a woman's needs sexually; he's *always* on the receiving end. Her needs don't mean shit! He can't hold out long enough for her to climax before he's nutted and ready to go to sleep. He doesn't care. He got *his*.

On the other hand, the woman, she's a control freak; sex is *always* on her terms. If it's daytime she wants, daytime, she gets . . . and there's no changing her mind. She makes a mere wimp out of her man. She gets off on the fact that he's whimpering and whining. He feels like a circus wrangler having to deal with all her antics! If he fails to comply, then he's assed out; she won't give him any! Unless she's in control, it's hard for her to climax during sex, unless it's *the exact way* she wants. She's the type that claims to have never had an orgasm and she's forty years old! Now, that's a damn shame! It's slightly her fault; all she had to do was let go! And she's gonna continue bruising a plethora of men in her path until she handles that shit!

Women that don't know their value in a thriving healthy relationship usually end up with very low self-esteem and become vulnerable to this type of man or woman. Once you are stuck, it takes years of counseling and the right kind of lovin' to both save them from further harmful abuse and repair the damage to their heart. Women that don't believe that they are special usually end up with very low self-esteem and become vulnerable to this type of man or woman. Some become prostitutes, drug users, or alcoholics, and it eventually leads some to suicide.

Codependent-type relationships in and of themselves sometimes bring a mental high to the players involved. Some people find joy in *always* having someone to depend on them. They would try to manipulate the stripes off a zebra! Sometimes men and women move in with their significant others to have a pseudo-mom/dad. Pseudo-Mom cooks and cleans; pseudo-Dad does yard work and pays the bills. All of this is bullshit, because no one is communicating anything… everyone is just using each other! If a woman or man brings something to the table that you can manage, it's a plus, not the fuckin' mega-million lottery! Don't get geeked because someone paid an electric bill or made you a casserole dish! Lean on your damn self!

Taste vs. Desire

You acquire taste for an individual through shared experiences, but *true* desire derives from the expectation of scandalous pleasure and total fulfilment. When two people meet, each person comes with their own set of idiosyncrasies that make them inimitable in the relationship dynamic. As you get to know someone, you begin to build flavor combinations—things you have in common. Although the palate is very sensitive, it can be trained. You might be an aficionado for multiplicity. Once you begin to recognize flavors *you* like, your senses become heightened with subsequent experiences.

Ever had drunken noodles? Green and red bell peppers, surrounded by a host of basil leaves, jalapenos and chicken, swimming in a sweet sauce! You gotta have it! Again and again! Once you have it—climax! That's desire! You can't manufacture it.

Remember: You learn how to taste with your tongue, eyes, nose, and your ears!

Have you ever eaten something you *didn't* like? Do you remember how repulsive it felt to your tongue? Your nose? You vowed never to eat that again, but in hard times, you *acquired* a taste for that which you didn't desire. The monkey ate green peppers when he was hungry; sound familiar? Your mind told you to ignore desire and go with what was *available*. That's the consequence people face when they fail to pay attention to *their* taste receptors! PLEASE! PLEASE! PLEASE! Pay attention to all *four* doors of perception…your body will thank you later!

Who said you had to cleanse your palate before trying something new? It's okay to intermingle in the development stage. Now, experiment and observe to *validate* it—yum! Later, you might encounter another individual that tastes *similar* to the former. The key word is *similar* because no one person has a fuckin' carbon copy, really. You still have the memory of the former *taste* with you, perceiving the new to be *better* in the same light. That's not always the case. So, in this new experience, you go with the wrong expectation and your mouth set for what? Disappointment. Damn!

Sadly, if you are hanging on to someone that you have an *acquired* taste for, you're just fulfilling D-U-T-Y. Desire only serves as a dirty dish rag! When you have an *acquired* taste for an individual that you've been with for a long-ass time ... you get used to things. That's what happens with most people. They have settled for the mediocre—someone they've been with for three, ten, or even thirty years—all the while desiring someone else. And what is duty? The duty is management. It doesn't matter if you get bored as fuck. Oftentimes, you're not the fire-starter and pretty much have become passive-aggressive on the issue of sex. I mean, you will *have* to show some sort of interest or things will get nutzo! You go with it ... and you manage to get off *sometimes*. That's the glue that kept you together.

Enter, desire ... your second wind. The reason you get up in the morning. *Acquired* taste is nice but you want to roll *all* over in desire. Desire gave you the fervor to restart your failing dental practice. And hope to believe in love and lust again. Supposedly, you were told that when you got older your taste receptors would age as you age. Desire destroyed that theory—definitely! Looks like your taste buds won't reduce; *that* plateau is limitless!

For some, they like to fuck (or make love with) the person they desire, then restart that shit at *home* with their *acquired*-taste individual, igniting fire from here to there. And that's okay if it's what works for you—in order to retain some sense of sanity. For others, it's ludicrous! Would you leave the *intense* heat of an industrial-strength oven to try to get warm under the *flicker* of a mere match? Nah! That's the power of desire; it's insatiable! You really can't get away from it. Its very nature leaves you spellbound and speechless at the same damn time! You could buy the *acquired*-taste individual a whole damn franchise of sexy lingerie or a truck load of designer suits, and it still won't compare to the magic of desire.

So what would happen if you were to lose a liking for the individual you call your *acquired* taste, and you *only* want desire? You have come to a pivotal moment. For years, you've just been going through the motions. Almost every sexual experience with *acquired* taste was mundane and boring—yet you managed to cope. Why bother? Now, you are here—and you've got some moves to make! Your *real* pleasures originated from the individual of your desire, and now that humble pie got you *head* first! And desire? He or she is no innocent party … being privy to the knowledge of your significant other—but doesn't he/she deserve doggone better! He/she is no "side-piece" as popular culture loudly brags about today. Don't let that garbage influence your decision. Whatever you do, remember this: Without desire, you will have a lifetime of regret and misery.

Sleeping Captain on a Sinking Ship

All your life you pray that God would allow you to meet someone that could rescue you from the troubled waters of life. Here comes the good-ship lollipop, commandeered by Captain Know-It-All. On the boat you go, without verifying a lick of trust... and leaving it all to that person. When disaster comes, you're ready to jump ship while the captain is oblivious and sleep. A true captain knows his/her role. He/she no doubt is oblivious to the engineer, crew, and anyone else on board for that matter. A true captain knows how to navigate calm and tumultuous weather. And it's common for boats to get small leaks, but those are unavoidable. So how did the boat get hijacked and sink—all on your watch? You were asleep... you ignorant prick! Why do most relationships end without so much as an explanation?

Boats Leak?

Yep. Did anyone ever tell you that you have a big-ass mouth? It's true indeed. Captain Know-It-All is runnin' his/her mouth, tellin' all the biz, makin' tiny pinholes in the relationship. All types of shit is getting in: drama, family, outsiders, etc. So now you have several, simultaneous leaks … all you need is for one to get enlarged enough to sink! Now, these leaks didn't occur overnight. Captain Know-It-All has been neglecting the relationship for quite some time and failed to patch them.

Having ignored forecasts of stormy weather, Captain Know-It-All is startled out of a deep sleep by waves crashing onto the deck. He/she stirs just enough to see what the clatter is about.

Highs & Lows

Waves are typical. Any type of ruckus can cause waves, i.e., misunderstanding, no communication, and withholding sex—stuff like that. Throw in your everyday environment (the wind) and you'll have constant highs and lows—got it? It's all in how you deal with it, too. No relationship is simple; each one has its own complex nature. If you can't deal, then you won't make it … and that's just the end all, be all. Why make a big fuss when the pressure you are dealing with is just life?!

The motion of the water can make any relationship rocky, no matter how perfect it appears on the surface. And when the boat gets to rockin' most people can't deal. They get dizziness, motion sickness, *and* vertigo—and that's a bit much! All of those relationship ailments come from having a lack of balance. Maybe you experience occasional dizzy spells from bringin' up the same shit over and over again. And when it hits you, you go into a tailspin! Or your motion sickness could be caused by trying to do too damn much simultaneously! Vertigo is the worst offender of them all! You're in the spin cycle and can't get out! Signs of the ailment are apparent, i.e., messy social media posts about fuckin' up your boy/girlfriend's mom/dad, fuckin' random men/women, etc.

How Do You Work This Thing?

Warning! Warning! Danger! Danger! Are you the kind of captain that would ignore *obvious* signs, or would you prep for potential disaster? There's nothing more reckless than a novice . . . someone who refuses to listen to reason, shuns any kind of wisdom or sensible logic. Now, that's a fool! Aside from that, the captain doesn't even know the nature of the job . . . his/her main role! So basically the captain is blundering . . . and your very life is in his/her hands. So there you sit, struggling to survive in hazardous conditions—with a captain who doesn't care about the safety of his/her passengers.

The passengers on board are depending on *you*—captain … "the expert." Just because you've been in the relationship "game" for ten, maybe twenty-plus years doesn't make you an expert captain in *your* role. It is a common saying that "experience is the best teacher," *but only fools enter that school.* Wisdom is the ability to *apply* knowledge. Many a so-called captain—male and female—have fucked up a good relationship with outdated information and equipment that's not worth a damn! Automatic and stick-shift vehicles operate differently: You have to use a clutch pedal and *constantly* switch gears with a stick shift; an automatic is more simplistic. With either type of vehicle, if you don't have a clue what you're doing, you can jack it up to costly repairs. The same thing can apply to your relationship: If you fail to operate/handle your companion with care, the damage will be costly and sometimes irreparable.

Rescue ME

You like wearing life jackets? Me, too! And that's just in case I *need* to be rescued. You know, I might accidentally fall out of the boat, or the boat might hit a tidal wave or a sharp metal object. Things happen. Did the captain pick you up on the dock or in the water? Were you smiling with delight as he/she whisked you into romantic bliss? Or were you smirking as Captain Save-a-Ho temporarily snatched you out of some ratchet love triangle?

BEWARE, CAPTAINS: not everyone that cries for help actually needs it!

Captain Save-a-Ho proudly wears his/her medals, boasting about all the men/women he/she has saved through the years. So what?! What's boasting and bragging ... when all you're doing is picking up alley cats/dogs? They are only there for the scraps! Can't you spot a pretender? They feign love and affection towards you. And, once all of that has been sucked up, or anything else for that matter, they leave you without any explanation. Sometimes you waste valuable months and years on a person who did not want rescuing. All the while, the faithful lady/man in waiting grows tired ... possibly getting rescued by someone else. Screw you ... you lose.

Hijack

The objective of all pirates is to steal valuables. If casualties are left behind, it's your own damn fault. When you broadcast vulnerabilities, i.e., what/when you're doing, how much sex you're *not* getting, how bad he/she treats you—when you broadcast news, it's no longer private. It becomes *everybody's* business! One thing about the eyes of a pirate is that they can spot a potential target afar off! They usually attack at night or early in the morning. After you've been targeted by a pirate, now he/she has to find a weak spot in you in order to make the hijack. Perhaps you let your boy/girlfriend go out alone to the same restaurant/club every Tuesday night, crying on the shoulder of another man/woman, constantly complaining about things being wrong. All of these things make you a *prime* target for pirates. They can smell gold—when you can't even see it! Do you think if you do *nothing*, the pirates might go away? Afraid not! Those pesky pirates usually are pretty sneaky and swift; once on board, it's hard to get them off without a fight!

Since pirates usually board at night or early in the morning, they are virtually invisible to your radar system. They come armed with the most innovative and lethal weaponry ... ready to fight *dirty*! The captain may appear valiant and strong amongst his/her crew, but if a pirate puts that whip appeal on him/her *hard*, surrender is imminent—for everyone! Pirates are ruthless and could care less how much work, effort, and time you put in ... just make way ... someone else is taking over! If you fight, you lose; if you don't fight, you still lose. It's a lose–lose situation!

Bizarre Obsessions

In the name of love, infatuation, etc., a lot of people have reduced themselves to mere emotional shreds—from following a girlfriend/boyfriend home from the club to obsessively calling a spouse every hour he/she is away from home. If the object of a person's desire is oblivious to this behavior or patronizes the individual, it will just cultivate their obsession and could easily turn volatile. Don't get it twisted: male and females can equally share the bizarre.

On the flip side, married couples can become obsessive over their spouses as well. Women that have an unhealthy attachment to their spouse, have the tendency to be needy, smother with affection, seek constant validation of love, and are very intimidated in the presence of other women around *their* man. Lady, we *know* that's *your* husband, but a marriage certificate and frilly panties does not a-keep him! In fact, you might run him away. It is quite annoying to see a woman that lacks confidence in herself, but namely her man. ... that she can't let him go as far as to the bathroom without checking his nutsack for lipstick. If "love" has reduced you to this behavior, then it's time to find a hobby or some other activity to attend to.

As destructive as obsession is, it can leave the individual feeling lonely, brokenhearted, and possibly suicidal. Oftentimes, the obsessed individual has tried to flip fatty spam into savory gumbo—yuck! For example, turning a one-night stand into a relationship, or misinterpreting a thank you card for something amorous. As fragile and unstable as the world's relationship climate is today, this is *not* the time to fuck with people's emotions. People now *will* seek revenge and have no qualms about maiming and murdering. You never know how *much* crap a person can deal with and how *long* they can take it. On the outside, they could be smiling, but on the inside, your ass is chopped! When you invest time (any time) in a relationship—whether it was in your mind or in reality—every one seeks a return on his/her "investment." Word to the wise: Don't fuck *anyone* that doesn't have as much to lose as you!

As women age, they struggle with dozens of insecurities and become consumed daily with those thoughts. One main obsession is the desire to remain young. Magazines are chock-full of articles like "20 is the New 50," "How to Increase Your Libido at 40," and "Pickup Lines for the 21st Century Cougar." They see skinny, scantily clad models on commercials with DD-size breasts, making them wish for augmentation surgery. If she's very insecure, then a routine trip to her male gynecologist might be uncomfortable, especially if he's attractive.

He, on the other hand, is just doing his job (examining her), while mentally she's having a mid-life crisis. As she lies on the exam table, she wonders: "Will I ever feel youthful again?" If she has a teenage daughter, who's prettier than she is, she is bound for a host of troubles! For example, some women try to recapture their youth through their daughter. A woman might start wearing her daughter's clothing, hanging around her daughter's friends—especially if there are young men around. She will start wearing revealing clothing that accentuates her best features. She *hopes* they are paying attention to *her*! She tries to be the life of the party with this younger crowd, namely the younger men. Her antics become more overt, desperate even! She might try to lure one of the young men with alcohol and possibly kiss them under the influence to gauge their response. If one of those men *happened* to be her daughter's boyfriend, she shoots and scores! She becomes so driven on recapturing her youth that she might fuck him as well.

Most men live in the past. When you put a group of men together, all they talk about is what they *had*. For example, men like to brag to other men about sexual exploits, being a former athlete, having an afro or other popular hairstyle.

Owning a '57 Chevy, '58 T-bird, '62 deuce and a quarter, '63 Chevy, or '65 GTO made them even more popular and attractive. Ahhh, yes! The glory days ... are gone! Now he's bald (or graying, if he still has hair), has a bum knee from an injury in college, drives a 2013 Ford Focus, and can barely scrape up enough energy for decent sex. Affection dissipates and romance wanes thin. In his youth, he could fuck her *all* day and niiiight ... good and plenty. Now, he's simply a night crawler that rolls over for a quick nut and goes to sleep ... no longer seeking to please her as he did in his younger days. He *still* thinks he's alright.

All About Me

Narcissists are all into themselves ... and your puny thoughts are simply at the bottom of the wish list. Forget about it! How did you hook up? Probably just some random dude/chick you met, ignoring all the "run away quickly" signs after that good lay they baited you with. Dummy! If you're willing to sacrifice dignity and time, then go ahead with your bad self, as my uncle would say! Narcissists are slickers, too! They have wonderful conversation, charisma, and designer bags or swanky watches—just to get a line!

Most narcissists are masters ... they aim to please and know how to get you on team ME! Step one is usually them emotions, so master pleasers will work on making you drunk *and* dizzy in bed! Yeah, baby, it's like that! The sex might be so intoxicating that it leaves your dick/pussy, fingers, and toes numb. Ha-ha! But, after that, it's back to the mirror of me for the narcissist! They just wanted to show you *how* they like it! You'll eventually spend the entire relationship apologizing for nothing you did wrong, striving to be on point 24-7, and being the daily winner of his/her insults.

Untrusting, Unforgiving

Paranoia needs medical intervention, but behaving out and out like an ass is revolting! So your last boy/girlfriend stole $5000 from your bank account—that's not me. And your wife/husband left you for a younger (say 2.0) version of you—that's not my fault. If your dog/cat gets run over by a disgruntled neighbor—why am I to blame? Your inability to trust, let go, and keep it movin' has nothing to do with me. It's all hinged on your wanting to be in control.

You can't control someone if they want to act crazy, dishonest, or even cold-hearted. People are just people. And, when you try to control them, you'll just lose control your-self! The next thing you know, you're trying to force people to apologize to you, to be your best friend, etc. It's all an act on your part. You only want to show the offender (and all would-be offenders) *how* a person hurt you, so you close the door to trust and forgiveness.

Each potential relationship ends in disaster because you scare him/her away with your erratic behavior. Walking around like a wounded warrior won't give you the Purple Heart! Sadness begets sadness. Lunacy begets lunacy. Blaming a loving mate for all your life woes is shameful! No one wants to waste time and energy on that!

Needy Nitpicker

If he/she says that she wants *you*, needs *you*—*you're* the air he/she breathes, the shimmer in his/her moon—and they constantly *show* you with action, believe them! Stop taking your mate through changes by having him/her prove his/her love to you. It's ridiculous! You have a quality man/woman. Check. He/she treats you well? Check. Doesn't beat your ass? Check. No verbal abuse? Check. Showers you with attention and affection? Check. Supports your hopes and dreams? Check. Is it good enough for you? Or are you out to find something wrong? Hold on tight, or forever be lonely!

Love Typo

Every human being at one time or another has been blindly infatuated or blissfully in love. Was it really love? Or did you make a typo somewhere? We could drown you in a plethora of songs, poems, etc., to get you in *that* memory zone. Getting hotter? Once dopamine gets tapped (and that's when you get aroused), you get focused, start chasing that high! We can get stuck in some screwed-up (and some healthy) relationships by dopamine. What's all this gobbledygook—and how can it help me with my relationship? It's a semi-possibility. Can you avoid *almost* all of the typos? Well, trying to avoid a love typo is like trying to sit through eight hours of a boring education lecture, hoping you make it through unscathed; that's not realistic. If you manage to avoid two out of three typos (which is rare), then you're a fucking *superhuman*! Um, check your blood please!

Setting Boundaries

Do you set emotional and physical boundaries, or do you allow any and every one to invade your precious space? Knowing how to say "no" is vital in having a healthy relationship. You existed as a bright, loving, and complete individual before you met him/her. Now, all of a sudden, you have a meltdown if he/she doesn't help you bathe your dog, Cisco … and Cisco is five years old! Who sets the boundaries? In the beginning of the relationship, you enjoyed talking for three to five hours a night; now all you want is a decent night's sleep after you get home from work. It doesn't take much to open your mouth to say: "Honey, I'm really tired. Goodnight!" You can remain very much in love with someone without getting *lost* in their world.

Giving Up Too Easy … Letting a Good Thing Go

Is it hard for you to accept that fact that you *have* a good woman/man? Do you constantly shy away from challenges when they arise in your relationship? How many times have you threatened to leave because it just because it seemed easier to be alone? Do you believe that if you just met someone new, all your problems would melt away? That's not reality! Keeping one foot cozy on a footrest while the other foot always has an airline ticket on standby does not make a good relationship!

If you have performed a loss-versus-gain analysis, and the gains outweigh the losses … I would rethink leaving. Unless you are under some type of intense physical or verbal abuse, which would cause mental and physical damage—if that's the case, then leave immediately!

You will not be a statistic and don't need to *be* the news for "love's sake." Any form of relationship *worth* having is going to take hard, tireless work. It's not a cakewalk! If the one you love is willing to make adjustments and assist you through challenges, then bravely meet him/her at the *same* level. Be willing to *fight* for the love you want.

Don't give up!

Immaturity

Every man is not a player and every woman is not a whore! Who told you that?! History gives people a bad reputation for their future—and that's the price you have to pay for previous naughty behavior. All things considered … people do grow up! Maturity is not an age thing; it's a mind thing. There are immature men/women from 18 to 100! I'm only dealing with adults here, as this is an *adult* conversation. However, vast amounts of men and women—in the twenty-first century—enter into relationships with an immature mentality.

Don't tell a person you "love" him/her—when you only "love" them as a friend—while sensing that their love goes *much* deeper! Be honest: Tell them that your love has not matured to that level yet. Do you know the emotional damage you can cause by toying with a person like that, especially when you add sex and intimacy into the mix? That man/woman thinks that by fulfilling you physically your heart will follow.

Um, if that was truth, then every man/woman you laid down with through the years would still be in love. Give me a fuckin' break!

Overly Religious

Jesus is on the main line ... uh-huh. But how many times do I need to hear that? How many prospective mates did you run away—Christian/non-Christian—acting like an absolute zealot?! Passion for Christ shouldn't mesh in the dating phase with a burgeoning love interest, really! Conversation should be simplistic and organic. When a person is enthusiastic about a topic, they tend to share too much at times. Take time getting to know someone ... pump the breaks if you have to! Slow. Down. This in no- wise means you're ashamed of your faith, just that you're using more wisdom in your application of it.

Finish the Job

id you come? That is the first question a male asks to his female partner. He yearns for this verbal gratification ... that he brought her to ecstasy. Ninety percent of women lie just to stroke the male ego. He rolls over, but before going to sleep, he continues to ask: "How was it?" "Was it Good?" "That was the bomb, baby!" Exasperated, she gets up, goes the shower with her magic wand, and finishes the job. Fantasizing about a former lover that took her *there*, she quickly reaches the climax that she has so desired. It's painfully obvious that only *she* knows how to pleasure herself. Is it even possible to tell him the truth? She's withheld the truth for multiple years ... that he *doesn't* satiate her sexual appetite. Now would be a good time to be a blabber mouth! Communication is key in any relationship. Instead of partners inquiring with one another about what pleases the other sexually, they make the general assumption: That what works on one person works for all.

Fulfillment is not about length, width, or depth, or whether it's five minutes or thirty minutes. It's how you *effectively* and *masterfully* utilize *what you have*. And that can only be accomplished through communicating what you like and what you dislike.

Do Your Homework

How in tune are you into your mate during sex? Foreplay? Does he/she squirm when your hands make towards the lower regions? Can you detect a sweet kiss versus a *hungry* kiss? How does your mate taste when you give him/her oral? Does your dirty talk arouse your mate, or does he/she wish you'd put a muzzle on it? Does he/she like you being a tease? Coy? Dominant/passive? Are you aware of how aroused your mate gets when he/she is giving? Receiving? These are questions you should be asking. And, if you can't answer six out of nine questions, then you really aren't a great study!

Relocating . . .

Sex in the bed can get boring and quick! You're sleeping in there damn near five to eight hours! With so many props in (and outside) your home, the possibilities and escapades are endless! Use your imagination. As you find your way to a chair, in front of a mirror, on a grassy knoll, or even back to the bed, keep this in mind: Amuse each other, laugh out *loud* if you will. You do have a sense of humor, don't you? Enjoy yourself at the same damn time! Ha!

Hello, Foreplay!

Okay, this goes back to doing your homework! Little to no foreplay can kill a man/woman's desire to even have sex period! Sparse foreplay is like a dentist giving you the bare minimum of Novocain—right before a drill hits your tooth! If my dentist did that to me, I'd want to dropkick him in the face! Agreed? No foreplay—um, I wouldn't ever wanna think about that! Perhaps, he/she is touching you in all the right places, but your arousal level is not where *you* want it to get the party poppin'.

Why bitch and moan now? What you've been accepting is some mediocre excuse! Not being nosy, but what is foreplay to you? It is *not* a dance routine, in which you follow the moves verbatim every time you hear the music! Foreplay is erogenous! Foreplay is exciting! Foreplay is freedom! Foreplay is not *selfish*!

Passionate kissing, sensual back/foot rubs, oral, and hand jobs are just a few things to strike arousal. Each and every individual is different. What's rough to me might feel wonderful to him/her. What's too soft might be not soft enough to another. Keep it vocal and visual ... be their hand guide! Don't be shy! Tell him/her *what you want!*

Now is not the time to put a muzzle on it! If what he/she is doing is *moan worthy*, give him/her that verbal affirmation!

Vroom Vroom, Lag Lag

Getting stuck in traffic is torture! You just want to hurry up and get home! Accelerate. Brake. Accelerate. Brake. Then, your leg starts to get numb from not being able to *consistently* accelerate ... yeah, that feeling! Can anybody find the rhythm? Fast? Slow? Somebody better figure it out, or else we all gonna be pissed!

Maybe he/she would prefer for you to come before him/her. If you're moving too fast, then you're not paying any attention. You've already climaxed and he/she is nowhere near close to one! Disappointed? Yep! You always will be. Some like to come simultaneously with their mate, and some wait until their mate finishes. Either way, find the rhythm and keep the beat!

Set the Mood

Candles are lovely and sensual music does create a romantic ambiance—but have you ever mixed it up and started things ass-backwards? Like cooking together while playfully mixing in some truth or dare or poker, where the loser has to strip stark-naked, stop cooking, and give you a hand job! Of course, wash your hands—you're cooking! You can always stop!

Don't Be Such a Prude!

Try it; you might like it! Okay, this is not applicable to every-one, but try and open up to letting down your inhibitions. Does the prospect of being spanked or whipped turn you on or freak you out? If your boy/girlfriend introduced a vibrator to you during sex, would it make you cringe or come *all* down your legs? Do you like touching yourself with a *live, active,* and *participative* audience of one? Lap dances, although sometimes awkward, can be an exhilarating event for both when nude. Sex toys are sold in an abundant vari-ety, so you are welcome to experimentation! Freedom from sexual inhibitions gives you two wonderful things: a mode of exploration and three men/women in one!

Pleasure in Play

So many women are sexually deprived in their marriages. In a non-Christian marriage, the woman may or may not be sexually inhibited. Christian women are taught to fulfill the man's desires and "just go with it." In the church world, married Christians are impressed upon with this passage of scripture:

> HEBREWS 13:4 – "Marriage is honorable in all and the bed undefiled"

Some couples take the *undefiled* component and go on to have a healthy marriage, while millions are in bondage sexually because some spiritual leaders have *added* taboos, or dos and don'ts to this passage of scripture, leaving millions sexually frustrated and ultimately unfulfilled.

In addition to this destructive interference, many spiritual leaders even had rules that, if members of the congregation were to engage in certain sex acts, they would be openly rebuked or excommunicated from that local assembly.

In this study, we would like to deal with how to bring sexual freedom to marriages again, by referring to the above scripture as our foundation. Because there are millions of sexually frustrated and unfulfilled Christians, they *may* seek and unwittingly discover another man/woman that brings them that *total* fulfillment. Now, wait! We are not talking about just two people coming together for sex … Here are a few definitions for your learning pleasure:

Adrenaline

- Makes you feel exhilarated
- Makes your heart beat overtime

Dopamine

- The brain's reward hormone
- Trigger for *all* addictions known to man
- Has highs and lows

Endorphins

- The brain's "feel good" and calming hormones, along with oxytocin
- Called the "bonding hormone"
- Hormone released before/through orgasm
- Suppressed by testosterone in men during sex

Phenethylamine (PEA)
- Triggers the release of the hormone dopamine
- Released at the peak of orgasm
- Found in chocolate
- Makes you feel overwhelmed with feelings of bliss, attraction, and excitement

Proclactin
- The brain's satisfaction hormone
- Makes you sleepy after sex

Many married couples will search and search for years trying to conjure relations with multiple sex partners to capture a "feeling" and still *never* find total pleasure. I think Mavis Staples said it best: "I'll take you *there*." Although, in a different context. Millions of Christian women and men have not been taken "there" in their marriages. This thing goes *deeper* than arousing the physical body and bringing someone to climax. It makes males (and females) repeatedly crave and yearn for another person sexually… an addict. The longer they go without, the more they repeat attempts to get it. And repetition shapes a tight bond. Caution: You might experience both highs and lows if you are in a complex relationship. For example, baby-mama drama, birth of children, a busy career, and being overweight. These are variables that cause a disconnect between partners. There are a lot of Christian husbands who have a twisted view on this, too. "She keeps coming back." Uh, that's not necessarily tied to dopamine.

Dopamine causes focus, *strong* emotional bonds, and feelings of elation. Have you asked yourself: Is she going through the motions or just trying to fulfill her wifely duties? Most men/women won't say anything initially, in fear of hurting their spouse's feelings . . . but eventually, the truth comes out. It might come out ugly, whereby he/she ends up in someone else's bed . . . so get focused! Without the dopamine *link* between you and the person you love, sex is merely like a mother trying to breastfeed another mother's baby—and that baby is already being breastfed! There's no bond. No connection. It's just sex.

Empty Love

Many marriages have suffered from years of monotony—whether it be the bedroom, dealing with children, employment, etc. Although the couples may have vowed to commit a lifetime to one another, commitment alone can cause feelings of depression and utter hopelessness. Commitment without passion will surely bring death to a marriage.

Cover What?

This chapter is primarily aimed at married Christians. Let's face it: Married Christians *have* a detestable rap in the news—it's embarrassing. In light of all the scandal in the news about married people cheating on their spouses, men/women hiding their homosexuality, or women being used as pulpit whores, it paints a grim light on Christian marriages everywhere. Who's being honest? No one! Everything is hidden because no one wants to come to terms about the *true* desires that lie within ... that gnaw at them daily.

So what happens when you truly wake up? You feel stirred ... invigorated!

The Awakening

It is time for married people all over to tap into an undiscovered area to bring spice back into their marriage. Because of the *undefiled* bed, married Christians can try:

- Watching an adult film with male and female performers only as *helpful* suggestions
- Visiting an erotic/adult sex store together to purchase sex toys, games, lube, etc.
- Watching your partner pleasure him/herself to climax while simultaneously pleasuring yourself.

NOTE: This is *not* for the shy, only the curious!

- Engaging in hot phone sex occasionally … just be visual and imaginative

WARNING: Sex toys can be *highly* addictive and *should not* serve as a substitute for your mate! Sex toys are just that—toys!

Fantasy Swap

It wouldn't kill you to indulge *just a little*? A smidgen? No one is a mind reader … I don't know what's going on in that twisted little mind of yours! Would you care to share? All of us are holding back something from our partner that's deep, dark, and lustfully sweet! Yes, *lustfully* sweet! Aside from the cheesy and gritty folklore we've all read (or seen) in some novel, TV show, porn flick, or online blog, there's something of our own we could share. Close your eyes, reach back into that kinky vault, and start swapping!

Ever told your spouse that you'd like to be blindfolded from start to finish—unable to see what your spouse is doing? The element of surprise and suspense wonderfully folded up together! It's sultry and mysterious, intriguing and sexually stimulating. Being that you're married, you *should* trust each other. If you feel that your spouse is taking things too far, *speak up!* Again, this is *your* fantasy that you are swapping with your spouse … if it's too damn creepy, you're welcome to skip it altogether!

Did the idea of a one-night stand scare you in your mid-twenties? Yup ... scared me, too! The prospect of runnin' up on an STD or HIV/AIDS doesn't scream "take my panties off" or "suck my dick"! You do have an option now that you're married: pretending to be strangers! You can up the heat and the ante with this fantasy—it's all up to how you *want* to play the game!

To make the fantasy more lifelike, you could meet up at a coffee shop and strike up a conversation and flirt with an *actual* stranger. As your spouse is watching, let him/her get an eye and ear full. The objective is to get your spouse's curiosity piqued about you. He/she needs to see that you've *still g*ot baiting skills! The observing spouse should try to start diverting his/her spouse's attention to him/her in some type of sneaky way.

Once the observing spouse has found his/her "in," he/she should go to work with equally verbal play—trying to persuade the pants/panties off the object of his/her affection. NOTE: You may have snagged your spouse eons ago with a corny/outdated pick-up line—or maybe even a clever one—but this time, you *must* come fully prepared with something innovative and modern! And, once you have him/her, putty for more, move in for the kill!

Take complete and utter control! Do what you want to do! No ropes or handcuffs necessary! How superior is *your* power of persuasion! Ravish me ... with all the intensity, wonderment, and fixation of all eyes on me ... sans the violent connotations of course! I want you. And you want me ... but you *have* to *take* it! No resistance, just *full* compliance! In shock and awe, I'll silently plead for more. Fantasy that?

Do you want to get your spouse drunk and take full advantage of them? If he/she can't hold liquor? Or gets tipsy or vomits too easily? Skip. You can always have one shot together and then pour a thimble full on your spouse. Experimentation and taste is up to you. Some prefer mixed drinks or hard liquor like vodka or brandy. Moscato is a very, very popular dessert wine with multiple flavor combinations. Wise tip: For this fantasy, let your wife get tipsy/drunk ... alcohol is a killer on the male sex drive!

Impromptu Quickies

Let's face it: Making love is endearing, draws us close to our spouses, and is altogether ... ahhh ... romantic. But sometimes you just want to fuck ... and that's okay! I mean, fuck whenever the mood suits *you*! No need to plan a damn thing ... just fuck! Throw in a little foreplay, and as soon as you *both* get turned on ... go for it! Don't talk, just fuck! If you're rambling, you're not fucking! Enjoy! It's a quickie, dammit!

Make Oral Your Best Friend!

Do you frustratingly count the minutes while giving/receiving oral? Or do you get lost in the moment while giving/receiving pleasure? When you're at work or driving on the road, do you wish your spouse's head was smack-dab between your legs? How much time has elapsed between the last time you've given/received oral? Three months ago? One year ago? Yikes! I would be climbing the walls with rock-climbing gear and scratching chalkboards at the same damn time! I pray that shit *never* happens to me!

When you make oral more of a chore than an ode to the one you love, you will *never* find enjoyment! What would make it more enjoyable for you? Frequency? Use of edible lubes, not honey/sugar. (Side bar: Adding too many "romance" sex-scene food additives = a recipe for a yeast infection or an allergic reaction! That would definitely kill the mood!) If there is something you do like about oral, hang onto that focal point for dear life ... and go from there. Enhance the moment!

Has he complained about your unwillingness to swallow? I mean, his diet has a lot to do with taste ... but you can communicate about that. You can experiment with foods that would change the bitter to sweet. If you are just unwilling, then damn! Moving on!

On the other hand, the female taste is a special combination of her diet, hygiene, and hormones. Umm, whoever you are, male/female, handle your shit in all fucking departments, please! No husband wants teeth on his dick and no wife wants a tongue forcefully shoved up her pussy! No blundering, please! I hate to keep reminding you that what you *won't* do someone else will—willingly and with artful skill!

It's a Party! It's a Party!

Dress the part all the time! Would you show up to the White House for a dinner in cut-off jeans, a halter top, and stilettos, brazenly showing off all your tattoos? Nah! Your ass would be in the most demure dress or cleanest suit, not a tattoo in sight. Why the hell do you go bed like you're about to work in the garden? It's not just the wives who get lazy wearing the flannel jammies and faded t-shirts; the men are not off the hook.

I think no one dresses for sex unless they know for absolute certain that *tonight's the night.* Why does it have to be the night? Can it be the day sometimes? Let's not use weight as an excuse for not dressing sexy. Sexy has nothing to do with weight. Big girls and boys can do the *damn thang,* hello! You are only as sexy as you feel!

Moving Forward

When being in love becomes disruptive to everyday living, it's time to evaluate your current situation and answer some hard questions. What brought you to this point? Could you move away from that man/woman and tolerate *not* being able to see them? Ever? Do you share mutual friends? Or do you live together? Do you text or talk via social media daily? Is he/she married or engaged? Again, these are just questions. Only you could answer questions specific to you. Each relationship has its own dynamic.

Wouldn't it seem fucking easy to just free yourself by divulging every detail of your aching heart to that man/woman? But to whose advantage? Theirs or yours? If the person is emotionally unavailable—and you knew it from jump—then you're just letting someone mind-fuck you. Yep! That's it. That's all. And all you get is sweet nothings that *never* materialize into anything solid. They are not free (at the moment) to give you the love you wholeheartedly deserve. What about *you* loving *you*—and extracting him/her from the equation? Ouch! Never thought of it? Chew on that! If all it was about the fucking, then you're good to go. He/she never made love to your mind; you're just connected by a person who knew how to *handle* you … moving on! You can always get laid!

On the contrary, if you had a genuine, extraordinary experience—that he/she has touched you so in your heart, body, and mind—you're *fucked*! Time to Google a relationship psychologist and start the process of disengaging. In the disengaging process, you just start letting go. Trust. The shit will be *hard*! Letting go is by far the hardest thing to do—and especially when you don't want to. It's something about the human will that can make a person behave very reluctantly. Sometimes people don't want to let go because they feel they have given so much and the person "owes" them. When you are plagued by memories, fantasies, and inanimate objects, e.g., movies, songs, cologne/perfume, clothing, this makes it even more difficult. Pieces of a former lover can remain with us in some way, form, or fashion.

Sometimes it's hard to cope, and our thoughts can even border on the obsessive. If people would just deal with real talk and stop saying, "I'm okay," when they really aren't. You are not deemed crazy if you talk with a psychologist about issues with love. This is your life, and there is only one you … you need to be healthy and whole for *you*! No man or woman is going to "complete" you! I don't give a shit (and neither should you) how wonderful they lay it down in the bed! Get real! You are not a fucking sex toy! Confidence and dignity are attractive ornaments…wear them with pride!

CPSIA information can be obtained at www.ICGtesting.com
Printed in the USA
LVOW07s0113280515

440144LV00001B/6/P